Embracing Change

Drako Sullivan

Order this book online at www.trafford.com
or email orders@trafford.com

Most Trafford titles are also available at major online book retailers.

© Copyright 2018 Drako Sullivan.

All rights reserved. No part of this publication may be reproduced, stored in a retrieval system, or transmitted, in any form or by any means, electronic, mechanical, photocopying, recording, or otherwise, without the written prior permission of the author.

Print information available on the last page.

ISBN: 978-1-4669-1825-2 (sc)
ISBN: 978-1-4669-1826-9 (hc)
ISBN: 978-1-4669-1827-6 (e)

Library of Congress Control Number: 2012903686

Because of the dynamic nature of the Internet, any web addresses or links contained in this book may have changed since publication and may no longer be valid. The views expressed in this work are solely those of the author and do not necessarily reflect the views of the publisher, and the publisher hereby disclaims any responsibility for them.

Any people depicted in stock imagery provided by Getty Images are models, and such images are being used for illustrative purposes only.
Certain stock imagery © Getty Images.

Trafford rev. 08/06/2018

 www.trafford.com

North America & international
toll-free: 1 888 232 4444 (USA & Canada)
fax: 812 355 4082

No one need fear death. We need fear only that we may die without having known our greatest power. -- *Norman Cousins*

Contents

Foreword by Ebony Robinson xi

Letter from Author xv

Introduction xxiii

Short Story 1

Testimony: Grateful, but Change Doesn't Come Easy ... 33

A Glimpse of My Past 40

Journal, 30 days 52

Goodbye Letter 71

Conclusion 77

Poem 81

Afterword by Sabrina Wingard 83

This book is dedicated to my children LaChyna, Londyn, DJ, and Jasmine; to all my nieces and nephews; to the children I have been able to be a positive influence on; Lay-Lay, Kobe, Jhylin, CJ, Kay-Kay, Michaela and Joseph; and to my family and friends who continue to support me. Thank you all so much!

Finally, in loving memory of my grandmother, Betty Sullivan. I love you and I still aim to make you proud of me.

Wisdom is knowing what to do next, skill is knowing how to do it, and virtue is doing it. – *David Starr*

Foreword by Ebony Robinson

Years ago, when Drako and I first met, we were two preteens running around the neighborhood without a care in the world. Well, at least I didn't have any. Drako, on the other hand, was worried about how to survive life in a world that wasn't so great for young men growing up in poverty. Even with me being there, I never knew exactly what Drako was dealing with. It was years later, after many letters, calls, and emails from the Federal Correctional Facilities, that I had a firsthand glimpse into his life. He, expressing his appreciation for life and how his hardships helped mold him, gave me inspiration to push harder. Drako took his time and used it wisely; from learning new trades, developing a new craft (leather), furthering his education, writing books, blogs, poems, and now participating in the Residential Drug Abuse Program.

When I found out about him signing up for RDAP and what it was about, I was happy for him. I was excited that he would have an opportunity to gain something that could make him better and prepare him for society. I witnessed some of Drako's struggles and circumstances that left him feeling that he had no choice but to hustle to take care of his family. Like many black families in the late eighties and nineties, his family was broken by drug addiction, leaving Drako to be the head of his household. Though life threw him lemons, Drako didn't gripe or complain, he just made lemonade. With all the obstacles in front of him, Drako didn't run and hide. He leaned in, met it head on, grabbed the bull by the horns, and truly embraced change. I have seen great improvement in him developing an understanding of what it takes to be a man. Drako has let nothing and no one get in the way of him being the best father, friend, and male role model that he intended to be. Embracing change isn't as easy as it sounds, and some will tell you it's the hardest thing you will ever do. Drako has truly exemplified what it means to really live a transformative life – life filled with purpose, understanding, patience, and most of all, love. No longer living a life full of negativity, Drako is well on his way to living life like it's golden by embracing change!

Knowledge will give you power, but character respect. – *Bruce Lee*

Dear Reader,

There will be moments when change can be unexpected and forced. You can plan and prepare yourself to the best of your ability but there is no preparation for the unexpected. Some things are beyond our control. You will never know what is held in the hearts of others and those very things that are concealed can have an impact on you. Especially, when hate, envy, and jealousy are directed toward you. These very things are the venom of negativity. During the time that I started writing *Embracing Change*, I was in a great space. Things were going well for me, so I figured it would be an appropriate time to share with others my transitions. I had planned to have this memoir completed in time for my graduation from the RDAP, the Residential Drug Abuse Program that I was participating in. My plan was to share it with Class 61, the class I was a part of. With all the programming behind me, I planned to focus on my writing and prepare myself to embrace a new world upon my release, a world that I had been absent from for nearly two decades. I was focused and determined to continue to build my character and embrace the changes that came to me.

Out of nowhere, negativity struck in the worst way for me and I found myself in a very frustrating situation. I had not done anything to warrant this perplexing circumstance. I had always adhered to the rules and regulations set forth by the correctional institutions that governed me. My prison record exemplified this. I had never had any type of disciplinary problems during my incarceration. I've always had a focus on doing whatever it took to get back to my family as soon as possible. With this being heavy on me, I made sure not to get involved in anything that could extend my stay in prison. So, when the K-2 contraband epidemic crash landed at this particular institution, I didn't have any worries. Or at least I thought I didn't. The authorities reacted, and this created an opportunity for the snake of negativity to release its venom. It was someone who wanted to cause me great discomfort and assassinate my character. Whatever the reason may have been, by putting me in the middle of something that I was not involved, it resulted in my being placed in the special housing unit (SHU) at this institution. Due to the poor form of investigation, I was shipped to another institution. Nothing I said or what other staff said on my behalf mattered. Everything that I had planned was changed dramatically. All that I had worked to accomplish in RDAP was lost. My character was tainted and worst of all, I was moved nine hours away from my family and friends, making visitation difficult.

These are changes that were forced on me and beyond my control. It caused me to have to practice what I have preached. I had to embrace the change and develop a positive attitude. I discovered the antidote to negativity's venom. I went to sleep with a positive thought and woke up with that same positive energy. Also, during this time another surprise came to me, a true blessing and one of the greatest gifts anyone could ask for. Finding out that I had a son was a balancing act for me. It helped me to deal with the negative energy that surrounded me and encouraged me to be positive. Reading the letter and seeing the picture brought me a great amount of joy. Looking at him and seeing a better version of me, touched me deeply and motivated me in ways that I can't explain. I had more reasons to push forward and stay positive. Once again, a change in my life had occurred and it was unexpected. I never knew and to think that this type of news came at a time when I needed to be motivated says a lot to me.

I became encouraged to embrace the change and be grateful for the blessings that I have. No matter how small or large, whether you view it as a good or bad thing, change is going to come. It is how you accept it that can shape your destiny. Be positive and embrace the change. Furthermore, know that a conscious mind doesn't cause problems; a conscious mind creates solutions. I hope and pray that my words encourage you. I hope that this brief reflection on one of the many turning points in my life will be a motivation or inspiration for you to find the courage to change your conditions within, just as it has done for me. To look in the mirror and realize that everything I want out of life is there for the taking. If I'm willing to admit that there is a problem, only then it can be solved. The only mistake that I can make in life is not correcting the ones I've made. Change comes every day and it comes in every form. See the change, feel the change, and know that it is for the greater good. Then, embrace the change to have a better life. I wish you well on your journey to the new you.

Sincerely,

Drako Sullivan

Your life does not get better by chance. It gets better by change. -- *Jim Rohn*

Introduction

This idea was inspired by my loved ones and friends that are supporting me during this lengthy time of incarceration. The motivation for this book came from Miss Sabrina Wingard who pointed me in the right direction. Just when I found myself surrounded by a wall of writers' block and needing something to write about, she suggested, "Why don't you write about your current situation. I am sure that people will like to hear how you have changed and some of what you have been through."

Thanks to her advice, *"Embracing Change"* was born. After that moment, my creative juices began to flow. I battled with how or what form that I wanted to share this story. I thought about writing a fictional story, but what I have and currently am experiencing is very real, so should the story be. I was a little hesitant about sharing my life or the things that I have been through. Then I realized that maybe my story, my many situations, and the tremendous losses that I've had to endure, helped guide me to the course that I am on today. I am on a course of change and on to a much better and healthier lifestyle. I hope that this inspires those who read this to embrace the change that can lead them to a much happier life. Change is always knocking at our door, it is up to us to allow that change to come in. I don't think that there is a human alive that doesn't want what is best out of life. Or at some point and time wished they were in a better place, state, or condition. I once read, the condition of a people will not change until they change the condition within themselves.

After being sentenced to Federal Prison for 262 months, I knew that I had to make a change. I knew that this was not what I wanted out of life, but I didn't know when or how that change was going to be made. So, I went to prison with a lot of anger inside. Bitterness and hate in my heart. It didn't take long for me to become institutionalized. I started to search for ways to fit in and a way to better do the time that I had in front of me. The thought of change never left my mind, I just wasn't committing to it. I knew that one of the conditions that lead me to prison was the lack of education. With change weighing heavy on my mind and in my heart, I looked for ways to better myself. I had dropped out of high school after the tenth grade. I got my GED in state prison, but I was forced to do so. South Carolina's state prison requires you to get it as part of the youth offenders program. I was there nine months and that planted a misconception in my mind of what prison was about. Once I got to Federal Prison, I wanted to change because not only had I seen the light, but I felt the heat. So, knowledge was very much wanted because I realized that in order for me to do better, I must know better. I went after any form of positive learning I could find. I took classes beyond classes and began to learn about me and what I really wanted out of life. Learning gave me a profound sense of hope and little did I know, I was on a voyage of change.

It wasn't until I opened my mind, I realized that I was responsible for me being in prison; not the guy who set me up, not the police, not the judges, and certainly not the correctional officer who was just there to do a job. Once I rid myself of the hate, anger, and bitterness that was in my heart; room was made for change, knowledge, and opportunity to find their way to me. Now, I have finally reached my last year in prison. It is very possible for me to be home next year before the holiday season of 2018. I can't explain the feeling that comes over me with the very thought of regaining my freedom. Not just because I'm going home and reuniting with my family but also because of the changes that I have made. I can honestly say that I am ready for another chance at a better life. I have overcome, persevered, and embraced change.

The best thing about the future is that is comes one day at a time. – *Abraham Lincoln*

Short Story

I decided to write a short story to share how I had a negative mindset against one of the, if not the best, programs I have ever participated in during my years of incarceration. The Residential Drug Abuse Program, better known as RDAP, is highly misconstrued and frowned upon throughout the system by inmates. The negative stories are passed along. Very few positive stories are shared. Many who speak against RDAP do not know a thing about it. I must confess that I was one of those individuals who ridiculed this program from the outside looking in. Now, I will be one of the first to say, this is one program every inmate should take before they are released. In RDAP, you are given tools to rationalize your thoughts, become conscious of your conditions, balance your lifestyle, successfully live with others, and begin a strong transition back into society.

This story is based on true events that had taken place prior to me signing up for RDAP.

Part 1 - Not Me

It is another one of those sleepless nights for me. Nothing bothered me more than the lack of respect that is given at this camp. It is two in the morning and these imbeciles are acting as if it is four in the afternoon. The sad thing is the only way I can get an intelligent conversation is to talk to myself. Something I found myself doing a lot of lately.

"What's wrong?" asked Mr. Conscience.

"I can't believe you just asked that stupid question," said Mr. Irritable.

"Try to stay positive," said Mr. Conscience.

"You been telling me that crap for years and what has it gotten me?" asked Mr. Irritable.

"You're at a camp now." stated Mr. Conscience.

"Psst . . . this is what you call it. Look out that window . . . What camp you know has a razor wire fence around it? Look at these pale, gray bunk beds and matching 3-foot lockers. And the only thing that is between these six by nine cubicles is 6-foot brick walls without any doors. Listen . . . do you hear that? That is a symphony of snores and farts!" complained Mr. Irritable.

"Change is coming . . ." Mr. Conscience began.

"Yeah, yeah, I know. It gets greater later. You've been saying that for years, too," interrupted Mr. Irritable.

"Things could be much worse," Mr. Conscience said.

"It could be, but I am not going to let it get to that," claimed Mr. Irritable.

"Well, it is good to see that we're still on our path to change," said Mr. Conscience.

"Yeah. . . .yeah . . . whatever," snapped Mr. Irritable.

"Just stay cool Drako," Mr. Conscience encouraged.

It was hard to find some sense of reason in this midst of madness. If it wasn't for talking to Mr. Harris or myself, I don't know what I would do for a conversation with substance. I have a lot of pain built up in me and it runs deep. It is hard not to be bitter after fifteen years in prison. The sad thing is, I didn't kill or rape anyone. I got all this time for drugs.

"Well, you were selling drugs for years and you did things you got away with," reasoned Mr. Conscience.

"That is my point. I didn't get caught," said Mr. Mollification.

"Just try to stay positive and out of trouble. Be grateful you're not back behind three fences with controlled movements and total chaos," said Mr. Conscience.

"I'm grateful but that don't mean I have to be happy. I am going to bid.¹ I am smart enough not to get caught up in any foolishness."

I was talking to myself again and trying to justify my bitterness. A part of me was trying to stay positive and be optimistic about my situation. I even considered signing up for RDAP, but I quickly dismissed that thought. I was able to talk myself to sleep, just as I had done so many times before. Change was heavy on my mind and it was starting to seem like I couldn't continue to run from it. I was starting to feel like there was a purpose for me to fulfill. But a major part of me didn't want the responsibility and that personality was now in control. So, I didn't think about what was to come. But deep inside, I was realizing I couldn't keep running from change. The morning came swift. I was awakened by the counselor's voice blasting through the intercom.

---

1   Prison slang for doing time to suit the inmate. An inmate's way of doing time comfortably.

"Attention in the camp! It's Wednesday. You know what it is! The recreation yard and education are closed! Report back to your housing unit and prepare for my inspection! No doubt, I'm in route!"

I laid there a minute and thought of how sick and tired I was of being in prison. I was disgusted by being around the same old things every day. Every week it was the same thing, everybody running around like headless pigeons. Just as I closed my eyes, in attempt to clear my head to get ready to face another day in this hell hole, I was interrupted.

"Yo, Drako."

"Wassup, Lil Hustle?" I replied to the gnat that was bugging me. He was known for trying to hustle everything he got his hands on.

"I got these milks. Stamp a piece[2]."

"Aight, I'll grab one after inspection."

---

2   U.S. Postal Stamps are used for currency in a lot of federal prisons.

One thing about prison, everybody think they have all the sense. All Lil Hustle was trying to do was get rid of everything he was not supposed to have. Now, if I had bought that from him and during inspection the counselor finds it, I am out of a stamp and a milk. It never fails. He always find something wrong with my cube. So, there is no need to give him another reason to scold me.

I was finally able to shake the load off and get going. Now that my bed was made, and my cube was in order, I had to get myself straight. So, I navigated my way through the pre-inspection chaos to the restrooms.

"Wassup, Toops?"

"Ain't much Drako. Just another day in paradise."

"I feel you. Which side are you cleaning first?"

"You can brush your teeth in the last sink over there," said Toops pointing to his right and walking out of the restroom.

I was alone, just me and the mirror.

"You just don't give up, do you?" I asked Mr. Conscience.

"Why should I?" replied Mr. Conscience.

"You say something Drako?" Toops asked, stepping back into the bathroom with a mop bucket.

"Naw, Bro, just talking to myself."

"Give me a hit of that. Ha, ha, ha."

I guess it tickled Toops that I told him the truth. I was about to give him a piece of my mind, but I let it go. He stepped out again and I was face to face with me. I stared in the only set of eyes that I could never lie to.

Buzzz! Buzzz! Buzzz! Buzzz! Buzzz!

I guess it was for the sake of aggravation. I think the counselor got a kick out of holding that buzzer the way he did every morning. I wondered if there was a method to his madness. I have seen people get comfortable in prison, believe it or not, and maybe the counselor had his ways of making sure that inmates don't get comfortable around him. He was enough reason alone for me not to ever want to come back to prison. So, I guess his aggravation is a good thing if it gives me something to think about before I think about committing a crime.

"Inspection people!" yelled the counselor walking in the housing unit.

"There he go with all his mess," mumbled one inmate.

"Yeah, all that ain't call for," said another.

"You're right, here I go! And tell me what ain't call for fat boi? You might've tried me! You better bring it in! Everybody by their cubes and no talking during my inspection."

Everything went quiet instantly and it amazed me how all these so-called tough guys just fell in line. Later, they all will be talking about how they run this and that. I noticed that the inspection was moving along pretty fast. It may be a good morning after all. Just when that thought crossed my mind, the counselor barged in my cube and started his ranting.

"I should've known. You are the only cube out of order. Look at this mess."

"My cube straight, Counselor."

"You can't slick the slicker! You see this string tied up over here, illegal. Too many shoes and they are not in a straight line, illegal. One book or bible is supposed to be on your locker, illegal! Three zero seven, is out of order! Mr. Sullivan, you are ILLEGAL!"

"Man, . . . Counselor . . ."

"Ah, ah . . . bring it in! Bring it in! I'll have you in that SHU so fast it will make your head spin. Now try me! Now get this pig pen in order!"

All I could do was shake my head and comply. There was no winning the argument anyway. I haven't seen anyone win one against the counselor and I wasn't going to be the next one to try. He went on his way and everyone else was spared, well, except for Lil Hustle. I guess he found his stash of milk and other food items he was stealing out of food service because he was letting him have it. I didn't feel so bad after hearing the tongue lashing he put on him.

I cleaned my cube to meet the counselor's approval. Fifteen minutes later, he announced the inspection was complete. I normally met my main man Mr. Harris at recreation for our daily spin around the track. I first met Mr. Harris at another prison many years ago, we were on our seventh year together at this point. He was at the end of a 22-year sentence. The sad thing was, it was his second time doing federal time. Mr. Harris was a realist and told you how it was. I liked that most about him. At the age of sixty, he is in better shape than most guys half his age. One thing that tickles me about Mr. Harris is he has this sarcastic way of accepting compliments. Whenever someone told him he looks good for his age, he would say, "Oh, I'm just trying to age gracefully." Then, he would follow that up with his slick laugh. I knew he would be one of the few that I stayed in touch with. Mr. Harris always made sense out of things that went on around us. To most folks, he was a grumpy, mean, and bitter old man. To me, he had a heart of gold and would do anything to help a friend. I think that prison gave him a good reason to be guarded. I found a way to connect with him and we have been friends ever since. As usual, he was high stepping around the track once I got to recreation.

"Hey Lil Bro!" he greeted, full of energy as always.

"Wassup Mr. Harris."

"I'm moving to RDAP sometime today."

"What? You . . .nah . . .You joking, right?"

"You know that I don't play them time jokes," he said in a humorous way.

"Yeah, but are you ready for snitch shack?" I said, laughing at my own joke.

"Hey, it won't bother me. I ain't giving them nothing to tell on me if that is the case."

"I know but I don't see being around that mess and doing all that silly stuff they do."

"You sound like these fools running around here. I don't care what they say about that program or what it is that I have to do."

"My bid is going too good and I ain't with changing it right now."

"Lil Bro, listen to me and you hear me good! It takes seven years to earn one year of "good time" credit. Now I can do that in nine months. I don't care what I have to do to get it. It makes perfect sense to me."

"You got a point there and I didn't look at it like that. So how much time will you have left once you are in?"

"You know what the monkey said when they cut off his tail?"

"No, what?"

"It ain't long now. Ha ha ha. I'll be out at the end of the year," said Mr. Harris, still laughing at his own joke.

I could see the joy sketched on his face. We just continued our walk and I didn't say much more about me not feeling RDAP. A far as I was concerned, one year wasn't worth all the hassle. My mind was made up and I didn't see it changing anytime soon.

Later that day, I helped Mr. Harris move his belongings into the unit that was assigned to RDAP. Just walking inside that unit made me sick. It looked like pre-school to me. It had decorations all over the place and it seems to be part of their brain washing scheme. I don't need to wake up seeing all that kindergarten stuff.

I had come this far, and I had done so much to help myself. I didn't see them giving me anything more that I would need. I felt that I could finish doing my time on my own.

In that unit, everyone seemed to be so happy and cheerful. I didn't understand how anyone could be this happy in prison. I walked by one room and they were all dancing. I couldn't believe seeing grow men doing the cupid shuffle.

"Come on in Mr. Sullivan," called out one of the DTS (Drug Treatment Specialist). I called her Mrs. Two-Step because she loves to line dance.

"No Ma'am, I'll pass. This ain't the place to be dancing," I said.

"You'll be doing it when you come move to RDAP," she said giving me the look of certainty.

"I don't see me moving down here."

"If you say so. We'll see. Have a good day, Mr. Sullivan," she said, getting back to her line dance.

I tried to get out of that unit as fast as I could, but I ran into another DTS. This one is a true southern belle. She had asked me before about moving to RDAP. I always made an excuse. She is known for getting her way.

"Hi there, Mr. Sullivan," she said with a heavy southern accent. "You moving in?"

"No Ma'am, I'm just here helping my buddy, Mr. Harris."

"Whatcha waiting on?" she asked with hands on her hip and giving me the look that she wasn't accepting any excuses.

"I don't know if it is for me," I said honestly.

"Hush that up. I'm going to get you in here because you need this. It will help you. We are going to talk about this more later."

"Yes Ma'am."

I agreed to talk to her and I knew that she wasn't going to let up. I just couldn't see it, after all the bull that I've heard they had to go through. I was set on doing my time the way that I wanted to do it. It was set in my mind that they were going to brainwash everyone else, but not me!

Part 2 What Is Willed; Will Be Done.

Time was really moving for Mr. Harris. It seemed like yesterday that I had helped him move in RDAP. This morning he told me that he was three weeks away from the final phase. I don't know where the last six months went, but I was happy for him. I was missing our morning walks, but it was good that Mr. Harris was programming to get out of prison as soon as he could. The funny thing was, I had heard that he was doing the hokey-pokey dance. I would have loved to see that.

I was able to find another way to spend my mornings by doing leather craft. I had gotten very good at it, too, and was making some very nice bags. The leather shop became my safe haven. It was a place that I could reflect on myself and my situation. Most of the time, I was there alone and was able to talk to myself freely.

"You have to have a plan, anything can happen now. Especially how laws are changing," said Mr. Conscience.

"I don't want to think about any laws, ain't nothing going to help," said Mr. Irritable.

"Why you gotta be so negative? If you want something you have to have faith and claim it."

"Man, I ain't got no help this far and I'm not going to start looking for any."

"We have to stay positive."

"I'm positive that once I am done with this time, I'll go home."

It was becoming harder and harder for me to stay positive with all the disappointments I was dealing with. I found myself in a lonely and dark place. I had just lost another one of my favorite people to cancer. There is no way to describe the pain that is felt when you lose a loved one. Now, imagine losing that loved one and not having a chance to say good-bye, a chance to see them for one last time, or a chance to grieve and reminisce with your family. Whatever pain felt at the time, you can multiply that by ten and that was what I felt like. It took six years for my pain to ease from the passing of my grandmother and now the loss of my Auntie Jan laid heavy on my heart. I distanced myself from other people to be alone in order to deal with the pain I had inside. So, I was consumed by my leather work and I hid in the leather shop as much as I could.

"Drako."

"Wassup, Raines," I answered to one of the few that I considered a friend.

"Man, the counselor been paging you. I knew you was trapped in this leather shop."

"Yeah, you know that I can't hear anything in here."

"Well, he sent me down here to let you know that he needs to see you."

"Aight, I'm on my way. Let me put these tools away."

I couldn't help but wonder what could the counselor want with me. I knew my cube was inspection ready and I hadn't done anything else. Maybe he had a form or something for me, I reasoned with myself as I made my way to his office.

Of all the things that my counselor could have wanted, nothing could have prepared me for the reason. His words crashed into me like a wrecking ball.

"Drako, your sister Sharika is in the intensive care unit. Your mom wanted you to call the hospital."

"Alright," was all I could say as my mind was trying to process what I just heard.

I cradled the phone in my sweaty palm as he dialed the number. I was in a trance, and my mind was racing. What could it possibly be? He made a gesture for me to take seat.

"Hello . . . Momma," my voice was already cracking.

"Hey, baby. How you doin?."

"I'm good Momma. What's wrong with Rika?"

"Baby, it's gonna be alright. It's gonna be alright," she said in between her tears.

Hearing my momma cry uncontrollably opened my flood gate of tears.

"Momma . . . Momma . . . what's wrong?"

"She may not make it. My baby not gon' make it."

"Momma, she gonna make it. Now please tell me what happen."

"It's her kidney and her liver went bad . . . it's my fault," Momma shouted and cried even harder.

Before I could comfort my mom or say something to try to encourage her, my counselor got my attention.

"It's count time," he whispered, "I'll let you call back after count."

I just nodded my head.

"Momma, I'll call back in a few. I love you Momma."

"I love you, too."

I could her hear her sniffles. I was at a loss for words as my heart tumbled to my stomach. I just hung up the phone and my head dropped low.

"Take some time to get yourself together," my counselor said as he watched my sobs consume me and my tears drench my cheeks. I could hear the empathy in his voice.

Once I got back to my cube, I began to question every reason for faith, every reason for living. If hope was given out in packs of cigarettes, I was on my last smoke.

She had been born with one kidney to begin with. I was on auto-pilot after hearing that news. I went back to my cube. I didn't want to be bothered. I asked how could a 29-year-old be in this type of condition? I didn't know what to think, but to learn that it came from alcohol abuse really devastated me. For the first time in years, I closed my eyes, allowed my tears to soak my pillow, and I prayed.

The rest of the week, all I could do was think about my sister, the rest of my family, and what they may be going through. Days were a blur for me. My sister wasn't getting any better and I was growing weaker from the fear of what seem to be the inevitable. The doctors gave up on my sister and gave her less than thirty days to live. It was at this time that I witnessed another side of my counselor. He showed genuine concern for me and my situation. He also had called a DTS to his office, Mrs. Two Step. She gave me some encouraging words. It surprised me that she stopped doing what she was doing to comfort me. Her words were comforting and of faith. For some, it may not have seemed like much, but for me it was the spark that I needed to relight my fire. *DON'T EVER GIVE UP* is what came to mind. It reminded me of when I first came to prison. I saw this picture of a crane eating a frog. The frog was able to get his hands around the crane's neck and he held on for dear life. It read, "DON'T EVER GIVE UP"! I was revived. I found a new sense of faith. I knew that what was willed, would be done.

I shared this fire with my sister. My counselor approved it for me to call as much as I could to talk to her. I used my 300 minutes that were allowed, and I called when my counselor had the time. He always made time. We talked about the future, we prayed, we laughed, and we reminisced about the past. We made a promise to each other to never drink alcohol again. We talked of hope for about two weeks or so. My sister found - through the strength of God, the love she has for her children, and from the love I was able to show - the will to live. She committed to change her life. I was able to witness the power of change and what it can do. To this very day my sister is alive and well. She is doing better each day. It helped me see that even with a job to do, there were people around me who actually cared for my well-being. The support that I received from the RDAP workers, helped me to see things in a different light. I saw the change that was made with Mr. Harris. I saw him go home with a new commitment to life. When I talk to him to this day, he is still sober and enjoying life. My sister was given a second chance at life. Mr. Harris had another chance to get it right and if I wanted it, my chance was there for the taking.

I was still hesitant, but I will never forget the day it happened. I was in one of my bitter moods and I was more disgusted with the everyday routine of prison. I remember it like it was yesterday. It was a Thursday morning and I didn't feel up to doing anything and I didn't want to be bothered. My plan was to go to the leather shop and hide. Just before I got ready to begin my day, my name was paged over the intercom for me to report to the RDAP unit. It was the voice of the straight shooter, the DTS that would tell it like it is. This morning her class was graduating, and she needed me to take photos because I was the camp photographer. I knew that "no" wasn't an option, but I went back to the unit pouting and complaining. I guess it was written all over my face because Raines noticed it.

"Hey, Drako, what's on your mind, Bro?" he asked out of concern.

"Man, I have to go take pictures of that stupid graduation."

"That is your job, right?" he asked rhetorically.

"You know that it is, man."

"Well, go do it and do it with a smile. You never know what may happen. It may change your day and get you in a better mood."

I knew that he had a good point and I tried to take a positive approach to it. So, I got dressed and got my mind set to do what I was getting paid to do. Once I got there, the atmosphere changed my mood and I lightened up a lot. I began seeing why these guys were always happy. They knew that they were getting closer to going home. It was one of the best ceremonies that I had seen since I had been here. The testimonies were real, and I could feel it. I don't know why this time it hit me, but it did. I left the graduation with a totally new perspective of RDAP. I couldn't wait to see my buddy Raines to thank him for his advice. My day was turned around and I had a different attitude from when I woke up.

Later that day, I was able to gain another perspective of the DTS that worked in RDAP; not that I thought they were bad people, but I thought they were there just for a check and government benefits. Even from Mrs. Straight Shooter, I was able to witness the concern and care that she had for the inmates in RDAP. I witnessed firsthand, her taking time out to help an inmate with some personal issues. It helped me to see even in the Bureau of Prison(BOP) there were people around me that actually cared for my well-being.

After Mrs. Straight Shooter called me to her office to thank me for taking the photos, I tried to make a speedy exit to get back to my unit, but I wasn't fast enough. I was stopped by Mrs. Southern Belle. There was no way to avoid her now and she seem to sense that she had me cornered.

"Hey Mr. Sullivan," she said in her southern accent. "How ya doin?"

"I'm doing pretty good, thank you. I am just on my way back upstairs."

"Oh, I see. You came and got you some extra cookies we gave out at graduation and now you rushing off," she shot at me, making me feel slightly guilty about being in a hurry.

"No, it's not like that."

"Oh really? What's it like then?" she asked with one hand on her hip and one eyebrow raised. "What is taking you so long to come to RDAP?"

"I'm just not ready yet," I said, trying to sound convincing.

"Not ready yet? You sound like you're making excuses. When is your release date?"

I knew right then and there, it was no escape. I didn't know what she had in mind, but I knew they had some people in RDAP now whose release date was later than mine.

"My year is 2020 ma'am," I said with some hesitation in my voice.

"What?? It is people down here with a 2022 release date. You should have been down here a long time ago," she said, looking at me as a mother would do when she is scolding her child. Before I could say anything, she was yelling down the hall for the coordinator of RDAP.

"Doctor, can you step over for a minute, please?"

Once the doctor came, Mrs. Southern Belle told her that I needed to be signed up for an interview. It was all out of my control at that point. The decision had been made and the next day I went through the procedure. I already knew that I was qualified for the program and I would get the year off. I moved into the RDAP unit September 23rd. The funny thing was that I moved in the same cube that Mr. Harris had when he was in RDAP.

I learned that you never know when change is going to come and how it will take over. It is up to me to embrace it and allow it to grow within me. I know that you can never say never. What is willed, will be done!

Dear Past,

Thank you for all the lessons.

Dear Future,

I'm now ready . . . - Author Unknown

Testimony: Grateful, but Change Doesn't Come Easy

It didn't take long for me to see that RDAP wasn't anything like what I had heard about. All the negative stories were mostly a misconception that was passed on. The unit at night was so quiet you could hear a mouse urinate on cotton. I had one of the best nights of sleep that I could ever remember in prison. Unlike the other units, everyone had respect at night. It was mostly because now was the time that guys started focusing on going home. In the RDAP unit, everyone showed caring and willingness to help out when it was needed. I couldn't believe that I was in the same prison. My first weekend was pleasant and a much-needed change.

The first day of class, I noticed that Class 61 was full of diversity - all ages, different cultures, and backgrounds. I liked that the class took a unified approach. We decided week one, that we would move as one. We were united in our goals to complete the program without anyone getting set back or kicked out.

There isn't much that I can share as far as the lessons we were taught but I will say that each module provided valuable information. A lot of tools were given for anyone open to receive it. For anyone with the opportunity to enroll in RDAP, I strongly suggest that you do.

I realized that I wasn't in just a drug abuse program, I was in a life changing program. If this wasn't true, I don't think that I would have been able to share the darkest moments of my past with total strangers. I wouldn't have found the courage to write about this wonderful change that I have embraced. Through it, I have learned to think more rational and how to take an honest look at myself. Now, I have a clearer vision on my life and the goals that I have set to achieve.

One thing you will read is my gratitude chain, something that we had to write as an exercise for our process group. Also, you will read the testimony that I have shared with Class 61 about my past. It is the reflection of my misdirection. I wrote this long before I decided to write this book. After the first couple of weeks, I was able to really see what RDAP was about. The stages that we had to go through made good sense to me. I was able to take a closer look at everything that I was required to do. I searched for the meaning and purpose in everything, from the morning meetings to different committees we had to join. I signed up for the newsletter committee.

I was able to get comfortable and suppress my negative self-talk. I opened my mind to all the good it could do from being honest and participating. Soon, I found myself looking forward to Wednesday - the day of process group. It put me in the mind of the twelve-step groups I use to go to with my mom. I never realized how much it could help talking about what was on your mind or things that you were experiencing while doing time. The starvation that I had for good conversation was satisfied. I discussed my issues and got positive feedback and some great advice. I developed an open ear for others, too. The assignments we got in Process Group were more like intervention for us to stay focused on our commitment to change and to help us develop empathy for others.

My gratitude chain consisted of the following seven things that I am grateful for:

1. I am thankful for the patience that I have because I know that it is a major part of the reason I have made it this far. Through patience, I have been able to humble myself and appreciate my blessings.

Embracing Change

2. I am thankful for my family and friends who support me because they have given me strength to push forward. Their support made things easier for me.

3. I am thankful for my good health and sound mind. After a long time of incarceration, people's health and mind goes. It is a blessing to have both after the many years that I have done. I am focused and ready to reenter society a better man.

4. I am grateful for my daughters, LaChyna and Jasmine. And my granddaughter Londyn. They are the fuel to my fire that burns inside of me! They are the very reason that I strive to be the very best that I can be.

5. I am thankful for another chance to change. Many have come and gone without the opportunity to make up for their mistakes. So,

I have every intention of making the very best of the chance that I have.

6. I am thankful that I am able to forgive those who I feel have wronged me. I pray that I am forgiven by those who I have wronged in my past lifestyle.

7. I am also grateful for the understanding that I am gaining from this experience and not letting it have a negative impact on my life but a positive one. Now, I am able to be responsible and think about my choices, so they don't lead to undesirable consequences.

Doing this exercise made me take a deeper look at the many blessings that I have. It helped me take time to appreciate life much more and to know that I have a lot to be grateful for.

My testimonial is a part of my journey to recovery. My recovery is not just from past alcohol and drug addictions, it's also from the lifestyle that I led and was in love with. I have heard that you must know where you come from in order to get to where you would like to be. I realized that you have to be honest in order to begin to change and you must see the error in your ways before you can correct them. Sharing is one of the many steps I have taken to embrace the change that I know will better my life and make me a better man.

A Glimpse of My Past

I was born August 16, 1977, in Greenville, South Carolina. In the beginning, my childhood was joyful in some ways and I believe that is due to the innocence that I was born with. I couldn't see how cruel the world was to my mother, being a single mother at sixteen. We were already poor and lived in a state of unbelievable poverty. Our house on Endel St. was shared with my Grandmother and two of my uncles.

By the time I turned four, my mother had given birth to my brother Jermany. At eight, my sister Sharika was born. By the time I was ten, Jerica had come into the world. My mother was in a very unhealthy relationship with my stepfather at the time. Our financial condition was very rough, and things were hard to maintain for my parents. They both were high school dropouts. My mother never had a regular job but Jerry, my stepfather, did. He worked hard for the hospital system as a janitor.

Early on, things weren't that bad as far as I could see. We were clothed and fed but that changed drastically. My parents started fighting more and more. We couldn't keep a stable home and we move around a lot. Once we lived with an uncle of my stepfather that ran a liquor house. I was exposed to a lot of the street life at an early age. I tried to ignore it, but I was drawn to it some way.

In 1986, crack cocaine crashed-landed in the south and that became my parent's drug of choice. From that moment, it seemed as if our little family started to unravel. It was an almost unbearable time in my life. I tried to escape through church but there was no hiding from the constant fighting and abuse that I witnessed my mother take. I saw my stepfather, a man that I respected, become defeated and robbed of his pride by his crack addiction. By 1989, my mother had decided that she just couldn't live with Jerry any more. Once they split, my mother relied more and more on crack and alcohol during these depressing times.

Since I was the oldest, she turned to me to help around the house and help with my siblings. She said that I was now the man of the house and I would have to help keep our family together. We were on welfare and needed public housing to have a place to live. Our house, in the projects of Piedmont Manor, became infested with crack users coming there to get high. It was the only way for my mom to feed her hunger for crack. Crack robbed me of the mom I knew and loved. Yes, I still loved my mother and had respect for her, but things weren't the same. Her addiction took total control. At the age of 13, I had to man up! It seemed that I was forced to do whatever it took to help bring food in the house. I worked whatever odd jobs I could; but at my age, there wasn't much that I could do. I loved school and I had dreams of playing professional basketball but that faded fast when reality smacked me in the face. I never wanted to sell drugs. In fact, I hated everything that had anything to do with drugs. Being so young made it hard for anyone to employ me, so in my young mind, I believed that I had no choice. I wanted to change our destitute situation, so I fell to the influence of peer pressure to make some "big bucks". In the spring of 1991, my career as a "dope dealer" began. In the beginning, I just wanted to make enough money to help take care of my family. My concern was Momma, Jermany, Sharika, and Jerica. They depended on me.

I didn't see this being the beginning of my demise. I was head strong and willing to do my very best in anything that I did. I did the same in the drug game. I was loyal to the streets. I didn't care what it took to make money. I did it. Having this attitude, gained a lot of trust from those who used me to sell drugs. It also put me in position to move up fast. I was given a lot of lucrative opportunities and, to a teenager, I felt that it was the best thing that could have happened to me. It led to my worst addictions ever - fast money, the lifestyle, and the reputation that came alone with being a drug dealer. Things were easy, and the money came fast. It was so good that this wrong seemed right and the abnormal seemed to be normal. I became deeper and deeper involved. I seem to be trapped in the very thing that I hated most. I became my own worst enemy. I pushed the very thing that tore my family apart and had my mother neglecting her children. I was on a fast track to where I am now - serving a 262-month sentence in federal prison. Knowing I was doing wrong and could come to prison, I did nothing to change. I loved it! I was just as much as an addict as those that I sold drugs to.

Seeing my family drinking and smoking marijuana gave me the impression that it was alright to do these things. At an early age, I became curious. At 12 years old, I took my first sip of vodka and stole a joint out of my mom's ashtray. By the time I was 14, I was smoking daily or whenever I could manage to get some weed. I was also running the streets and selling drugs without any adult supervision. My mom was too far gone. Her addiction had the best of her. I felt everything was all on me, and to my knowledge my step-dad was worse than my mother. I was my own parent and I had three siblings to look after. The streets now had my mom and myself in its vice grip. At 16, I was either drunk or high everyday just to cope with the overwhelming responsibilities. I was lost in a very dark and cold world. The only way for me to survive was to become dark and cold right along with it.

My mom is an addict and to this very day she struggles with her addiction to crack, alcohol, and marijuana. That is over 30 years of battling these demons. As for my stepfather, he was able to get his life on track and he's still very close to us all. He is taking the steps needed to stay sober. I just pray that he continues because we all know that it doesn't take much to slip back into darkness. I appreciate that he has not given up on my mom and tries to encourage her to get sober.

I wished I could have been a better example for my siblings. My brother followed closely in my footsteps. I know that he is responsible for his own actions, but I can't help but feel that it is my fault for the road he had to travel. I am just grateful that he is getting his life together. As for my sisters, they were only 14 and 12 when I came to prison, so it was the same as me leaving my own children behind. I feel that I left them to take care of themselves. It is not surprising that they turned to alcohol and drugs. I just encourage them to think about their future and the future of their children.

My sister Sharika, which is next to the youngest, nearly lost her life to alcohol. In the spring of 2014, she was hospitalized for kidney and liver failure. Doctors had given her less than 30 days to live. But by the grace of God and her will to live, she pulled through. Now, she knows that she must stay sober or die! I made a promise with her to never drink alcohol again, a promise that I have no intention of breaking.

My younger sister has her own share of problems. She is also caught on escaping her situations by drinking alcohol and getting high. I pray that I am able to reach her before things get too far out of control. She has two beautiful children that will be affected the most by her actions. I do feel responsible for my siblings. I also think that had I not come to prison things would have been different for them. Despite the exposure to drugs and alcohol abuse, my family managed to keep a tight bond.

We have a tough time showing our love but we all know that it is there.

Every relationship that I have, either intimate or platonic, I approach with a positive attitude. The few relationships that I have are very positive and supportive. I do have some amazing people in my corner and those are the ones that I know are my real and true friends. I am very grateful and appreciative of all that is done to make this situation as easy as possible. It is a blessing to have someone to turn to when you are incarcerated. They are just as excited as I am about me being in RDAP. They encourage me to continue to do my best and stay focused.

I now realize that my actions not only hurt me, but they hurt my family and friends in ways that I could never imagine. I know that by coming to prison, I took a pillar of family away from them. The one person that they depended on most, was now in prison. I neglected my responsibilities of being an example and leader to my loves ones. Thinking that I was doing something to make things better for us as a family, only made things much worse. There is no amount of money that can fix what I have broken with my poor choices. Even now, after 15 years, my family is still suffering from me being in prison.

What I have lost due to my loyalty to the streets, thirst for alcohol, my craving for marijuana, and the lust for the lifestyle that came with being a dope dealer - has cost me tremendously. What I have paid has been immeasurable and there is no way to get that back. I have spent nearly 16 years in prison now and I have missed some of the most precious times of my children's lives. I can never relive the birthdays and graduations. Just to think that there are some things that I would have given my life for, now seems I have given most of it away, for nothing. I now realize that my loyalty was to the wrong thing and wrong people for all the wrong reasons. I can only hope that my family forgives me for the pain and worry that I have brought to them.

In conclusion of my brief testimony, there are not enough words or time in a day to express the pain that I feel and the remorse that I have for what I've done. There are so many people that love me and care about me and I have put them through some tough times. I now see that I was very selfish. I never took the time to think about the end results of my actions. I pray that I am given an opportunity to express my deepest apologies to those who were affected by my actions. For me, there is no greater pain than the one that is self-inflicted. This is why I am so committed to being better and doing better for the purpose of living better!

You must be the change you want to

see in the world. – Gandhi

Journal, 30 days

We are required to keep a journal to touch on some of our daily activities or emotions we may be experiencing each day.

I now regret not keeping one the entire time that I have been incarcerated. I mostly wrote and expressed things that I was feeling that day. Going back to read it from time to time, helps me stay focused on the things that I want to achieve moving forward in my life. I hope that you are able to notice the growth as I was able to. It is such a great feeling when you can see the fruit of your labor. Things are so much easier to deal with when you are honest and positive.

If you are serious about changing your conditions, a journal, in my opinion, is an effective way to record and analyze your progress. It doesn't take much time, just a few minutes a day to write down your thoughts or feelings. It could be something that you did or something that has happened to cause you to feel a certain way. Whatever the reason is, be sure to write it down. Remember, honesty is the key. For me, keeping a journal has been therapy. Maybe it can do the same for you.

September 27, 2016

I continue to realize that my assumption of RDAP prior to me signing up and moving into the RDAP unit, was completely wrong. Ever since Friday, the day I moved in, it has been a pleasant experience. I have absolutely no complaints. I also realize that this was a much-needed change. It is like a breath of fresh air.

September 28, 2016

Today was my first process group and it was another awakening experience. It gave me a chance to work on participating and sharing. Something that I felt would be a struggle for me. *You never know what you need until you get it.* (My thought for the day)

September 29, 2016

Today in class, I had to write some issues that I felt that I have and set some goals on how I plan to address them. Things are starting to make sense to me. I was able to be honest with myself. I have trust issues and I don't like socializing with just anyone. Now that I have my issues written down, I can begin to correct them or at least make an attempt to. Another good day!

September 30, 2016

I have been sharing with family and friends about me being in RDAP. I felt that they would be very supportive and today I received an email that really moved me. Sometimes, even when I know that I am doing the right thing, it is good to hear someone tell you that they are proud of you. It motivates me to continue to keep pushing forward and working hard. That email was a reminder for me to keep positive people around me who encourage, motivate, and inspire me to stay focused and be positive.

October 1, 2016

Today I got a surprise visit. My significant other and her mother came to see me. It was great to see her and sit and talk with her mother. It was a good feeling. It showed me that this is a very healthy relationship and we are growing closer. Our relationship is getting stronger. It gives me so much joy to know that I have so much love and support in a situation like this.

October 2, 2016

Today I had another great visit. My significant other and I were able talk about our expectation of one another. Some things we disagree on, but our conversation was constructive and positive. *Communication is 2% talking and 98% listening.* (My thought of the day).

October 3, 2016

Today was a long day for me. It wasn't bad, just long. I showed a little willingness today and played flag football. I really enjoyed myself but one thing I realized is that I am not as young as I use to be. But the fun and the relaxation that came from it is what mattered most.

October 4, 2016

Today was another long day for me. For some reason, I couldn't get it together. Class wasn't making it any better. It was so boring sitting there and having to listen to people talk about their past. After break, I took a different approach and tried to think positive. And after hearing some other's testimony, I was able to appreciate my many blessings. My day ended a little better than it started.

October 5, 2016

Today was pretty good for me. Process group was very good. There was a lot of sharing and great feedback given. I am starting to feel more comfortable with the idea of sharing with people that I don't know that well. It is coming along a lot sooner than I thought it would. I guess taking the advice of my buddy Tovis Raines is helping. He told me to give it a chance and think positive about it.

October 6, 2016

Another good day for me, I contribute it to the positive attitude that I have adopted. Class was great. I realized something else today, it helps to listen to others when they give their testimony. It is 9:00 pm now. My day didn't end the way it started. Well, it was still good but I was feeling down when I didn't see my name on the list for those who received clemency. I am happy for those who did receive it but very disappointed to not get it when I feel that I deserve it.

October 7, 2016

Today is one of those days that I am really sick of being in prison. I don't feel like being bothered or being around anyone. I thought that I would have been out of this slump by the end of the day but I am not. I am going to write or try to do something to shake this negative energy.

October 8, 2016

I hate to blame it on anything, but I have to blame this mood that I am in on the rain. I am down and feeling more home sick than usual. This morning, I chose not to let it get to me. I did my best to put forth a positive attitude and doing that helped me have a better day. But I am still ready to go home.

October 9, 2016

Man, time is really flying for me. I can't believe that it has been three weeks since I have been in RDAP. Things are really moving in all the right directions for me. I believe that it is going to be another great week.

October 10, 2016

Today I got to myself just to have a moment of reflection. So, I walked around the track and thought about being home and the small things I once overlooked, like being in the park enjoying the beautiful weather that we had today. So today I got another reason to stay focused on the much-needed change to give me a better and happier life.

October 11, 2016

On a scale of 1-10, today for me was a seven. Not really much going on, but it wasn't a bad or negative day. I am grateful for that. I am really trying to put a positive foot forward and keep it there. Tomorrow is process group, but I am not really looking forward to it because I am not really into sharing my life or problems with people. I guess I will have to see how it goes.

October 12, 2016

Today was a very negative day, or at least in my thoughts. I had to really ask myself what do I want, and do I really want this change? I had to ask myself this because I thought about signing out of the program. I believe that the devil was hard at work. I know that I want better for myself. I know that I must change to get it. After soul searching, I know that I can do this program. I see that there may be some tools that I can take with me. I just have to stay focused and go get it!

October 13, 2016

Yesterday in process group, the DTS brought to my attention that I was struggling with being institutionalized and trapped in the very system that I hate. She told me that I couldn't take this type of behavior to the outside world. Today in the morning meeting, I had to address the issues in front of the whole community. I got a lot of positive feedback. I was showed some things that I didn't think was a problem. It was good to get others' opinions. This was a morning meeting I will always remember. Thought of the day, *don't knock it until you have tried it.*

October 14, 2016

Today I got a wonderful surprise. I got a visit from someone special. It really took me to a peaceful place and it was great to spend time with a beautiful lady. I am feeling the love that I am getting. I am very grateful for the support that I have. I appreciate every bit of it.

October 15, 2016

I have been going nonstop since I've been in RDAP and haven't had time for me. So today I decided to have this for me. I just chilled out and relaxed. I watched some

TV and enjoyed my night. What I got from this is that I must have some type of balance in my life so that I won't become overwhelmed or stressed out.

October 16, 2016

I had another wonderful visit today. I am always grateful for that. Today marks my 15th year in prison. Looking back, I can honestly say that I am a much better man than I was when I first started this sentence. I just pray for the strength to continue to push forward. I have an opportunity to change and make a difference. That is exactly what I plan to do.

October 17, 2016

I know from doing time in prison that anytime your days are moving so fast that it is hard for you to keep count, you are doing "good time". I am really starting to enjoy my classes. I don't know if it because I love learning something new or if it is just being in RDAP. It is really helping me do my time better. For anyone who doesn't have much to do in prison, my advice is to sign up for RDAP. My thought for the day is to stay focused and stay driven.

October 18, 2016

Today the DTS in charge of my class started things off a little different and it helped set a positive tone. It made the class fun and now I have something else to look forward to. We started the class off with a positive thought or quote. I know that I can't expect for every class to be this exciting, but I can still have a positive approach to it. Today was a good day.

October 19, 2016

I talked to my mom today and it was so great to hear her voice. It lets me know that she is doing fine. She was excited about her trip to Vegas. I am happy that my mother is going places and doing things differently. I hope that it helps with her addiction. I love to hear of her trying to make a change for the better. She told me that she now has her permit and soon will try for her license. For my mom to be doing that, shows progress. My thought of the day, *it is never too late for change.*

October 20, 2016

Today was my first time addressing the community. I had to get up and conduct the community business. By doing this, it is helping me with my public speaking. This is something that I plan to do once I am out of prison. I was nervous. I don't think that I did too bad, but I am going to work hard on getting better.

October 21, 2016

I am just feeling really good today and I hope that I have many more days like this. Now I am wishing that I would have come to RDAP sooner. That is funny to even think that way. I think that this program should be available to everyone that is serving a federal sentence. It can help make things much better.

October 22, 2016

Today I just read, Wh*o Moved My Cheese*, and it was a great read for me. It helped me to look at some things in a different way. I related most to the character Haw. It made me think back to times when I could have reacted sooner to changes that I faced. I may have had a totally different outcome.

October 23, 2016

I had to stay positive today. It wasn't a bad day, but it wasn't a good one either. I am just focusing on what is to come and making sure that I stay committed to this change I am on. I want to do better. I want a better life. This is what I have to tell myself to help deal with the negativity around me.

October 24, 2016

I practiced being open minded today and took a class on finance. I really enjoyed the first class. I am looking forward to gaining more information that can help me focus on my finances. Today I noticed that this program has a lot to offer. I just wish it was available to everyone.

October 25, 2016

Today was a hard day for me. I realized just how much my daughter Chyna needs me out there. I am very disturbed by this. I had to reflect on the choices I made that caused me to not be there. It helps me to really look at how important this change is for me and how I must stay committed. I have no choice. My family and my children need me. I deserve to give myself a better chance at life and they deserve a better version of me.

October 26, 2016

I had process group today. I am finally seeing how talking about things and sharing what may be on your mind can help you better deal with situations. I never thought that I would be able to open up to strangers. But I did and was given some good advice about some of the things I was dealing with. Lesson learned today - it is best to get things out than to hold them in and let it eat away at you.

I am grateful to be able to share with you the entries of my first thirty days of RDAP. I was able to let go of some frustration and see my change in progress. I encourage anyone to keep a journal. It can become your best friend. What I thought would be too much work for me and a big aggravation, turned out to be easy and therapeutic. Just like that old saying goes, "don't knock it until you try it". Change comes to you in all shapes and sizes. Focus on being positive and embrace the change that is to come.

Don't live the same year 75 times and call it a life. -- Robin Sharma

Goodbye Letter

I have come to realize that when embracing change, old things must be let go wholeheartedly. You have to really want it. Change is something that must come from within. Your situation will never be better unless you change. You must take a look at yourself and figure out what is holding you back from having the life that you want to live. That is what I was doing. In RDAP, we were given an assignment to write a letter to say goodbye to the very things that held us back. I wrote one to say goodbye to my addiction and the criminal lifestyle that I would have died for. I would like to share it with you. I hope that this encourages you to take a similar step toward change that I have. I really hope that you are willing to let go of the dead weight that is slowing you down from being great! It is time to say goodbye!

Dear Lady Alcohol and Ms. Criminal Lifestyle,

Before you two say it, I already know. It has been a long time since we've spoken. Yes, we had a lot of fun together and been to a lot of wonderful and exciting places. But I have to be honest and say that I don't miss it one bit! I have come to realize that you two never meant me any good whatsoever. All you ever gave me was false hope and foolish pride. Yeah, you two made it seem like my best interest was in mind, but it was only meant to keep me trapped in a world of darkness.

Lady Alcohol, I think back to our first kiss. I was only twelve. I snuck you out of my mother's sight and for some strange reason after the bitter taste, I came back for more. It took a couple of years for us to hook up again, but we hung out every weekend after that. You being there for me when I was struggling with my issues made me feel that you were really down for me. At times, you made me feel invincible and gave me unbelievable courage to speak the truth. You helped me discover parts of me that I have never known. But the whole time you were poisoning my mind and eating me from the inside out. Destroying my dreams! And just when I was about to break away from you, you brought me back by sparking my interest in a threesome with your friend Ms. Criminal Lifestyle.

You knew that she would keep us together. I was blinded by all her glitter and gold. She brought to me things that I never thought that I would be able to have, but it was all a false sense of happiness. I know that she is a liar and doesn't care about me at all. I am sure that she has found many to use after me. Lady Alcohol, I know that it is in your nature to ruin lives. When we first met, I was a child and I was very weak but even as an adult you were able to keep your hooks in me. I am proud to scream that I am finally free! You will never have the pleasure of ever being with me again! I now know who I am and all the pain you are able to cause. Thanks to you and your trusted friend Ms. Criminal Lifestyle, with all the ill advice, I have paid a tremendous price. By following your lead, I found myself trapped in prison. My children have grown up without me and my family has been torn to pieces. Most importantly, I have disappointed me! So, this will be the last time that you two will ever hear from me! I have a fresh start and I am embracing change. I can live for my family and me! I will not let you two disrupt my road to recovery! I wrote this letter to the both of you. I know that Ms. Criminal Lifestyle is not far from you Lady Alcohol, so pass this on . . . I have moved on to a better me and a healthier lifestyle.

Love me no more,

Drako

At times, I reread this just to remind me that life is all about our beliefs and the choices that we make. Change is a must to have a better life than the one that you are living when nothing you do seems to be right. It is hard to do the same thing day in and day out and expect something new to come to you. If you want anything out of life, you can't wish for it, you must work for it. Jim Rohn said, "a better life doesn't come by chance, it comes by change".

What we, the colored people want is character. And this nobody can give us. It is something we must earn for ourselves. -- Frederick Douglass

Conclusion

My journey can never become your journey and the paths that I have traveled will be much different than yours. Although we may have taken similar routes, our destinations will also be at a different place and time. I can only hope that our destiny is a positive and blessed one.

In life, I have realized that there is no such thing as a smooth road or an easy way out. Life's terrains are rough and has its share of changes. You won't be able to predict every turn, every stop, or delay. You won't know how long the trip will be. One thing for certain, there will be all sorts of changes along the way. Some may be chosen, some may be forced. It is all on you how you deal with the changes that come your way. You can prepare yourself by making sure you have all that is required and still there are no guarantees that it will be an easy voyage. Life has its road blocks, speed bumps, traffic jams, and potholes that can interrupt your travels. What makes a difference, is how you react to it. I recognized that in order for me to have an opportunity at a better life, I had to be honest that change was needed. I had to see the change and I had to embrace the change. I sincerely hope that I have inspired others to embark on a journey that leads to change.

Life was never meant to be easy. Trials and tribulations have been occurring since the beginning of time. Everyone will have to face their own hardships. It may come from their conditions or choices that they have made. Many things we feel are mistakes are really bad decisions we have made. Our actions after the terrible decisions is what makes the difference. The only bad decision that is everlasting is the one that is made when you decide not to correct the bad decisions you once made. In order to correct situations, you must change your self-thoughts and your attitude that support these self-thoughts. If you continue to have an irrational approach to life, you will lose every time. You must believe that there is a better way. You must act on this belief. No matter what you desire out of life, you must put in the work to get it. You cannot wish it to come or wait on someone to hand deliver it to you. You must get up and go get it!

Changing your condition starts with realizing that there is a problem. You must find the source of that problem, whether it be a bad habit, a close friend, or your perspective. Once that is done, you must work on a solution.

My life took an undesirable course and I was left shipwrecked. Once I realized that I am the captain of my ship, I was able to get things back in order and pursue my journey - a voyage to a better life and honest living. I know that whatever destination I reach, from this point on, I am solely responsible. I must make better decisions to have a better life. You are the captain of your ship! Where do you want to go? What do you want out of this life? How do you want to be remembered? Now is the time for change. It is there for you, so embrace it! If you have gotten nothing else out of this book, please take this with you: NOTHING IS OUT OF YOUR REACH, IF YOU JUST TAKE YOUR HANDS OUT OF YOUR POCKETS!

Embracing Change

Life has its uncertainties,
and there is only one guarantee.
That is . . . what will be . . . will be.
But change comes with endless possibilities.

Change is the start of your journey.
A journey to reach your destiny.
Change can be what you need
to make your dreams a reality.
Change comes with many opportunities.

Your reaction to change will be the key.
Changing within is the first step to succeed.
Positive change trumps all negativity.
Change must be done with sincere honesty.

Afterword by Sabrina Wingard

Just as some of the things I once held strong to had started to fade, he helped me believe again!

The most captivating thing about, *Embracing Change*, is that at some point in life, everyone should make the decision to do just that! Even as a child, Drako was embracing change. His life story is so inspiring and can be so comforting for anyone facing challenges from being in this very same position. At some point, you or someone you may know, have been in his shoes. Him allowing readers to come into his world and experience in depth what he has experienced is growth. He takes you through a few stages of his life, good and bad.

Today, Drako has accepted full responsibility for all of his actions from his past, is paying his debt to society, and is focused solely on being a better Drako and moving forward with his life. He is focused on being a better grandfather, father, uncle, brother, son, and an overall positive role model for our future leaders of the world. He is always positive and has managed to remain that way through everything he has been through. It has been an immense pleasure seeing Drako grow and embrace the many changes that have come his way.

Drako has inspired me in many ways. His courage to embrace change and his ambitious personality has allowed me to view situations, as he would always say to me, "as if the glass is half full versus half empty". Prompting me to remember that optimism will create opportunities while pessimism finds a way to kill the opportunity. He's shared some of the things he has learned throughout his growth process to help me continue to grow as well. I truly appreciate his tenacious efforts to continue to reflect positive energy into the universe and I look forward to watching him continue to flourish in his future endeavors.

Made in United States
Orlando, FL
11 January 2024